PARABLES OF JESUS

Steven Mueller

CPH
SAINT LOUIS

Edited by Thomas J. Doyle
This publication is available in braille and in large print for the visually impaired.
Write to the Library for the Blind, 1333 S. Kirkwood Rd., St. Louis, MO 63122-7295;
or call 1-800-433-3954.

CONTENTS

INTRODUCTION TO LIFE OF JESUS

Life of Jesus explores the ministry and teachings of Jesus. Each study in this series includes twelve sessions addressing topics related to the study's theme. Life of Jesus gives Christians the opportunity to get "up close and personal" with the person and work of Jesus as they study God's Word and discuss applications to their lives with other Christians.

Life of Jesus uses a simple, user-friendly format consisting of four major components: Focus, Inform, Connect, and Vision.

Focus — introduces the participants to the concepts that will be explored during the session.

Inform — guides participants into Scripture to learn what God says about different issues.

Connect — provides activities and questions to help participants apply the truths found in Scripture to their lives.

Vision — suggests activities for additional growth during the week to come.

Life of Jesus can be used with large Bible study groups, in small groups, and by individuals as they seek to enrich their devotional life.

The accompanying Leaders Guide provides a suggested format for study and answers to questions.

May God strengthen you in the faith as you study His Word using Life of Jesus.

READING THE PARABLES

FOCUS

When we read the Gospels, we see the wonderful things that our Savior has done for us. We see His perfect life, His innocent death, and His glorious resurrection. We know that He did all this for us and saved us by His work. We see another facet of Jesus' ministry as well: we see Him as our teacher. One of the common teaching methods He used was the parable. Some of our favorite Bible stories may be parables. What are parables? How do we understand them? These are the questions we examine in this session.

Jesus taught people using many parables. What are some of your favorite parables? Why?

INFORM

Read Matthew 13:34–35.

a. How did Jesus teach the crowd in Matthew 13? What does Matthew point out about Jesus' use of this teaching method?

Read Matthew 13:33.

b. A parable is, in essence, a comparison. It uses a common earthly event to reveal a spiritual truth. What is the earthly event used in this short parable? Can you think of other common events or activities that Jesus uses in parables?

Read Matthew 13:24, 31, 33.

c. But a parable doesn't stop with the earthly story. It points us to some spiritual truth. What do these verses say the parables revealed?

Read Matthew 13:33 again.

d. While some parables are more detailed than others, they all
    have a main point. What do you think is the point of this brief
    parable?

Read Mark 4:10–12.

e. This challenging passage shows another truth about parables.
    What do unbelievers see in the parables? What might they not
    see?

f. Since this is true, what do we need to understand the parables?

CONNECT

Parables utilize a concrete, earthly story and compare it to a truth
about the kingdom of God. They have one main point, but are often
puzzling. Most importantly, we need to read them with faith. Let's consider these qualities as we study two brief parables.

Read Matthew 13:44–46.

a. These two parables have the same point. What is the earthly
    situation in these parables?

b. Who do you think the people in these parables represent?

VISION

God has richly blessed us in so many ways. He created us. He
redeems us through Jesus and calls us to faith by the Holy Spirit. He even
takes the time to teach us more about Himself through the parables.

Since God has chosen to teach us through the parables, how
will we react to them?

Session 2

THE PRODIGAL SON
(Luke 15:11–32)

FOCUS

It is a familiar old story. We see an estranged family. Poor choices were made by different family members, behavior is bad, hearts are unforgiving, and old grudges get in the way. One family member has to hit rock bottom before he changes. What is this? Just another tragic story? The latest TV miniseries? No, it is a parable told by Jesus that helps us understand more about ourselves and our faith.

Strained family relationships are all too common in our society. What advice would you give to a friend who was estranged from his family?

INFORM

Read Luke 15:11–12.

a. The younger son made a request of his father. What did he want? What was wrong with his request?

Read Luke 15:13–16.

b. How did he use his inheritance? See also verse 30.

c. What happened when the inheritance was gone? What impact did this have on the young man?

Read Luke 15:17–21.

d. Verse 17 is the turning point of the whole story. The younger son saw what he had done and repented. What words describe his repentance? How do these words accurately describe sin and repentance?

e. Having realized his failure, he resolved to return to his father. What was his attitude in returning home? How does this indicate a change of heart?

Read Luke 15:22–27.

f. The father heard his son's request and then answered. What did the father do and say that was beyond any reasonable expectation?

Read Luke 15:28–32.

g. How did the older brother respond to these events? Did he have a point? Where did he go wrong?

h. How did the father respond to the older brother?

CONNECT

a. Many people call this parable one of their favorite parts of the Bible. This story is easy to identify with because we can see ourselves in it. How have we been like the younger brother?

b. If we stop with the younger brother, we may miss an important aspect of the story. How are we like the older brother?

c. How does our heavenly Father bring us back to His family? What place do we have in that family?

VISION

We know this story. It is precious to many Christians because it is our story. We have acted like both of these sons. God is like the Father. He has never stopped loving us, and He brings us back into His family. But this story does not depict a one-time event. We fall into sin every day, and daily our Father forgives us and welcomes us back.

a. What can we do when we fall into sin again?

b. The older brother in this parable did not want to welcome his brother back. How can we rejoice when others believe?

Session 3

THE GREAT BANQUET
(Luke 14:16–24)

FOCUS

Imagine that a great and famous person, whom you like and respect, is throwing a party and decides to invite you to attend. Not only does he or she invite you; you are provided with everything you need. Your transportation, lodging, and even your clothes are provided for you. How would you respond to this invitation? Would there be anything that might keep you from going? What would you do to get ready?

INFORM

Read Luke 14:16–17.

a. The man in this parable prepared a great banquet. What kind of preparations do you think he made?

b. The Bible describes heaven as a banquet. Here God prepares everything. What kind of preparations has God made in heaven? See also John 14:2–3.

Read Luke 14:18–20.

c. What excuses were offered for not attending the banquet? What do you think of them?

Read Luke 14:21–24.

d. When his invitation was declined, the man decided to invite others. What two groups did he invite to his banquet?

e. How many people did the man want at this banquet? Why?

10

f. How do you think these guests reacted when they were brought to the banquet?

g. What happened to those who rejected the invitation to the banquet?

CONNECT

a. The meaning of this parable is clear. God is like the man holding a banquet. He invites all to the heavenly banquet, a banquet that will last for eternity. How is this invitation rejected?

b. What excuses do people offer to God?

c. Who are we in this parable? Are we those invited first or those invited later?

VISION

"Sir . . . there is still room." The master in this parable sent out his servants until the banquet was full. This is true of the heavenly banquet as well. There is still room. God, our Master, sends us out as His servants to invite more people to the banquet. There is room enough for all in our Father's kingdom.

What can we do to invite more people to the banquet of salvation?

Session 4

THE TALENTS
(Matthew 25:14–30)

FOCUS

In this parable, a master gave his servants a number of "talents" to use on his behalf. We might conservatively estimate the value of one talent as more than $10,000. Some servants used his money wisely, but one did not. What would you do if someone entrusted you with a large sum of money? How would you react? Would you eagerly take on the job, or would you be afraid of the consequences if you mishandled the money?

INFORM

Read Matthew 25:14–18.

a. Jesus tells us about a man who went on a journey. What preparations did he make for this trip?

b. Why do you think he gave different amounts of money (talents) to different people?

c. What did his servants do with the money in his absence?

Read Matthew 25:19–23.

d. How did the first two servants perform? What did the master tell them?

Read Matthew 25:24–30.

e. What was the excuse of the third servant? How did the master respond to the excuse?

f. Looking at the whole story, do you think the master was wise
    in trusting his money to these servants?

CONNECT

a. Jesus tells us that this story is a description of the kingdom of
    heaven. He is the Master and we are the servants. What "jour-
    ney" has God gone on?

b. Before the master left on his journey, he entrusted his property
    to his servants. What has God entrusted to us? What does He
    desire us to do with these things?

c. What came first, the work of the servants or the gift of the master?
    How is this like our Christian life?

VISION

Our Master and Savior has truly blessed us. He is with us and gives
us all things freely. We have received so much from His graciousness. He
loves us so much that He even gives us opportunities to serve Him and
other people in His name.

a. What gifts has God entrusted to you?

b. What challenge for service has God placed before you today?
    How will you respond?

Session 5

THE SOWER
(Mark 4:1–9, 14–20)

FOCUS

God has blessed us beyond our imagination through Jesus Christ. Through our Savior, we have freely received life, forgiveness, and eternal salvation. So why doesn't everyone believe? If it is possible to reject God's blessings, is it possible that we might fall away from the faith? These are the questions asked and answered by Jesus in the parable of the sower.

a. Why do you think that some people do not believe in Christ?

b. What is the difference between Christians and non-Christians?

INFORM

Read Mark 4:1–9, 14.

a. This parable uses the picture of the sower to teach us. What do the sower, the seed, and the ground represent?

Read Mark 4:15–20.

b. Some of the seed falls on the "path." Whom does the path represent? What happens when these people hear the Word?

c. Some seed falls in the "rocky places." What happens to the grain planted there? What do the rocky places symbolize?

d. The third type of ground has thorns growing on it. What happens when seed is planted there? How are some people like thorny ground?

e. The final type of ground is the good soil. What happens when seed is planted there? What kind of people does this describe?

f. Why do you think the sower in this parable doesn't limit his seed to the good soil? What does this tell us about God's plan for us?

CONNECT

a. This parable is about different kinds of people. It also describes each one of us. When have we been like the path?

b. We've also been like the rocky soil. We need depth in our spiritual life. How do we get it?

c. This parable talks about thorns choking out the Word. All people have some thorns in their lives. What threatens to choke our faith?

d. How can we be like good soil?

VISION

The prophet Isaiah writes, "So is My word that goes out from My mouth: It will not return to Me empty, but will accomplish what I desire and achieve the purpose for which I sent it" (Isaiah 55:11). That is the promise of God. When His Word is spread, it will always accomplish something. In the language of this parable: God's Word will always bring a harvest.

a. What kind of crop do we produce as good soil?

b. Who is responsible for "sowing seed" today?

Session 6

THE UNMERCIFUL SERVANT
(Matthew 18:21–35)

FOCUS

What do you do with a person who just will not change? They hurt you and apologize for what they have done, but then they do the same thing again and again. It doesn't take long to get frustrated with such a person. Finally we say, "Enough!" Or perhaps we forgive them, but hold a grudge. We watch very carefully to make sure that they can't hurt us again. But is this the way that God wants us to be? That is the question raised by this parable.

a. How many times do you think we should have to forgive another person?

b. How many times do you think that you should be forgiven when you do something wrong?

c. Is there a difference between your answers? Why or why not?

INFORM

Read Matthew 18:21–22.

a. Peter asked Jesus if it was enough to forgive someone seven times. What do you think of Peter's question?

b. How often did Jesus say that we are to forgive? What was Jesus trying to teach Peter (and us)?

Read Matthew 18:23–25.

c. Jesus taught about forgiveness through the actions of this man. He owed his king 10,000 talents—millions of dollars—and couldn't repay. How did the king propose to settle this debt? What do you think of this plan?

Read Matthew 18:26–28.

d. What did the indebted man promise his king? Do you think this was a realistic promise?

e. How did the king respond to the plea of the debtor? Why do you think he did this?

Read Matthew 18:29–35.

f. After receiving this amazing gift, the man found himself in a
   situation of reversed roles. He found another man who owed
   him a few hundred denarii—a fraction of what he had owed
   the king. How did the man deal with his debtor?

g. How did the king respond when he heard how his servant had
   acted?

Read Matthew 18:21–22 again.

h. After hearing this parable, what do you think of Peter's question
   and Jesus' answer? How is this parable really Jesus' answer?

CONNECT

We might see ourselves in this Bible story. We have asked questions like Peter's. We also can see that we are like the servant and God is like the king.

a. What debt do we owe to God? How has He responded?

b. What small "debts" might others owe us? Do we try to hold
   them to a higher standard than we are held?

c. How often does God forgive us? How often do we need to forgive others?

VISION

To forgive is simple, but not easy. It is hard for us to overcome our sinful pride to forgive others. It is hard to forget the sins committed against us. But that is the will of our God. Jesus taught us to pray ". . . and forgive our trespasses as we forgive those who trespass against us ." Thank God that He does forgive us and helps us to forgive other people.

a. What motivates us to forgive?

b. Privately think of a person that you need to forgive. Remember
   that Christ Jesus died for her/him, just as He died for you. He
   has forgiven you. Now, motivated by Jesus' love for you, forgive
   that sister or brother!

Session 7

THE LOST SHEEP AND THE LOST COIN
(Luke 15:1–10)

FOCUS

Have you ever lost something that was very important to you? What did you do? Did you look for a little while and then give up? Did you ask for help in finding it? Or maybe you can remember a time when you were lost. How does it feel to be lost?

a. Share a time when you were lost or lost something precious.

b. What did you feel during this time?

c. How did the situation end?

INFORM

Read Luke 15:1–2.

a. Why were the Pharisees upset with Jesus?

Read Luke 15:3–7.

b. This parable begins with a problem. What was wrong? Was this really a big deal? How did the man in the parable respond to the problem?

c. What did the man do with the rest of his sheep while he looked for the lost one? Was this responsible behavior?

d. What did the man do when he found his lost sheep?

e. How is the story of the lost sheep similar to our human condi-
tion?

f. What happens in heaven when a sinner repents? What does
this tell us?

Read Luke 15:8–10.

g. How is this parable similar to the first one?

CONNECT

a. These parables are really about us. When were we lost? Whose
fault is it that we were lost? See also Isaiah 53:6.

b. At the beginning of these verses, the Pharisees were upset that
Jesus was eating with tax collectors and sinners. What do you
think He was trying to teach them in these parables? How does
this apply to us?

c. Jesus taught that heaven rejoices when one sinner repents. How
does it feel to know that heaven rejoices over you? What does
this tell us about our worth in God's eyes?

VISION

This parable is about us. We were lost, but Christ has found us
and brought us back to His flock, the Church. But there are other people
who do not yet know Jesus as their Savior. Jesus has not given up on
them, but continues to offer His grace and forgiveness.

a. How can we help people who are still lost in sin?

b. How do we react when a sinner repents and believes the
Gospel?

Session 8

The Rich Fool
(Luke 12:13–21)

FOCUS

Most people go through life with a series of goals in mind. Maybe they have consciously adopted their goals. Perhaps their goals have never been spoken. Goals give us direction and guidance. If we meet them, we might consider ourselves successful. If we accomplish a worthwhile task, we feel like a success. But what is success?

    a. How do you think our world normally defines success?

    b. What things does the world fail to consider when it considers someone a success?

    c. How do you think God measures success?

INFORM

Read Luke 12:13–15.

    a. This story opens with a request from someone in the crowd. What did he want? Why do you think Jesus answered in the way that He did?

    b. In response to this question, Jesus gives us a warning. What does He warn against?

    c. This man wanted a greater share of an inheritance. What riches did he already have?

Read Luke 12:16–19.

    d. How was the man in this parable successful?

e. This man worked very hard to reach this level of success. When did he plan to slow down and enjoy himself?

Read Luke 12:20–21.

f. Why did the man's plan fail?

g. In the end, was this man rich or poor?

CONNECT

Read Matthew 6:19–21.

a. How does God measure success?

b. Is it wrong for a Christian to have money and other possessions?

c. What does it mean to be rich towards God? See also Matthew 6:33.

VISION

You have probably seen the bumper sticker that reads "He who dies with the most toys wins." Perhaps you have also seen the response: "He who dies with the most toys still dies." There is nothing wrong with money or possessions, but Scripture teaches us that "the love of money is a root of all kinds of evil" (1 Timothy 6:10).

a. How can Christians use the possessions that God has given them to glorify Him?

b. What can we do to place God first in our lives?

THE PHARISEE AND THE TAX COLLECTOR
(Luke 18:9–14)

FOCUS

"I'd go to church, but the roof would fall in on me."

"I couldn't go there. All the people would look down on me and judge me."

"Why should I go to church? Everyone there is a hypocrite anyway!"

Have you ever heard statements like these? They are among the reasons that people give for not going to church. Even if they are incorrect, they still represent a perception that many people have.

a. Why do people feel like they will be judged if they come to church?

b. How can we make it easier for them to come?

INFORM

Read Luke 18:9–12.

a. What was the content of the Pharisee's prayer?

b. Was he really different from the people he mentioned? Do you think he was ignoring any sins?

c. About what was he really praying?

Read Luke 18:13–14.

d. How was the tax collector's prayer different from the Pharisee's?

e. Which prayer was pleasing to God? How do we know this?

f. How were the positions of the Pharisee and the tax collector reversed in the end?

CONNECT

a. Luke 18:9 says that this parable was spoken to people who were confident of their own righteousness and looked down on others. Does this ever describe us?

b. Read Isaiah 64:6. Why can't we boast of our own righteousness?

c. What does God desire our attitude toward other people and their sins to be like?

d. What is our attitude before God?

VISION

Sadly, many people still have the attitude of the Pharisee. They quickly condemn other people and act as if they are righteous and holy by their own actions. This is false, and it is wrong. God calls us to a humble faith like that of the tax collector—a faith that trusts in and receives God's mercy.

What can we do to have a more welcoming church?

Session 10

THE GOOD SAMARITAN
(Luke 10:25–37)

FOCUS

As Christians, we know that we are supposed to love our neighbor. But this is easier said than done. Some people seem so difficult to love. Are there any exceptions? Who is our neighbor? Do we really have to love everybody? How is that possible? What about strangers—how are we to treat them? These are the questions raised in this familiar parable.

a. What kind of people does our society find most difficult to love?

b. Who is easiest to love?

c. What makes the difference between these two groups?

INFORM

Read Luke 10:25–27.

a. What question did the man ask Jesus? What was wrong with his question?

b. How did Jesus answer his question? What do you think of His answer?

c. Can anyone really do what the Law insists on?

Read Luke 10:28–37.

Notice that Luke shows us that this man was not righteous; he was self-righteous! He "wanted to justify himself" (verse 29).

d. Priests and Levites were religious leaders who worked in the temple. How did they respond when they saw the injured man? Why do you think they acted this way?

e. Samaritans were outcasts. The man Jesus was talking to probably hated Samaritans. How did this Samaritan outdo the priest and the Levite?

f. Undoubtedly, both the priest and the Levite thought they loved their neighbor. What made the Samaritan different?

g. What do you think is the main theme of the story?

CONNECT

a. The man questioning Jesus knew that he was to love his neighbor, but he tried to impose limits. He didn't want to include all people as his neighbors. Do we ever try to limit our service and God's love?

b. The hero of this story was a Samaritan. It is ironic that a person who was rejected and hated by many people should be the only person in the story who behaved appropriately. Who are the Samaritans in our community? How do we respond to them?

c. Jesus tells us to love God with all our heart, soul, strength, and mind, and to love our neighbors as ourselves. He tells us to love people absolutely. Are we able to accomplish these things? Who is?

VISION

This parable boldly proclaims two truths to us: we are to love God, and we are to love our fellow human beings. We cannot limit our love to any one group. We are to share His love with all people.

a. Does our church ever seem to limit God's love? How can we be more open to people who are different from us?

b. Who is the neighbor God wants us to reach today?

WORKERS IN THE VINEYARD
(Matthew 20:1–16)

FOCUS

"It's not fair! I work with a group of people, and I do most of the work, but we all are paid the same. My co-workers don't pull their own weight. Isn't it obvious to my employer that I should be making more money than those slackers?" How many times have you heard questions like that? Workers can be very concerned with issues of fairness. Everyone wants to get what they deserve.

a. How do you react when you are cheated or treated unfairly?

b. How do you react when you receive something good that you didn't earn or deserve?

INFORM

Read Matthew 20:1 7.

a. A vineyard owner went to hire workers for his vineyard. What wage did he promise to the workers?

b. When did the vineyard owner start hiring workers? When did he stop hiring?

Read Matthew 20:8–10.

c. The owner arranged for payment at the end of the day. Who were the first to be paid? Do you think they were surprised by what they received?

d. Did those hired at the beginning of the day have a right to expect more?

Read Matthew 20:11–15.

e. How did the workers hired early in the day react when they were paid?

f. Was the vineyard owner fair with his workers?

Read Luke 23:38–43.

g. For how long did the second criminal follow Jesus? Did Jesus
    treat him fairly?

CONNECT

The vineyard owner was generous with those he hired last. But he
was also generous with those he hired first! He did not have to use
any of these workers. He did not owe them anything. God is like the
vineyard owner and we are like the workers. None of us deserve God's
gifts, most of all the gift of salvation, but He gives them anyway.

a. Does God bless those who come to faith later in their lives?
    How?

b. If God will bless us late in life, why shouldn't we wait to
    believe? Why not live a sinful life first and then convert later?

c. How does the child of God react when someone comes to
    faith?

VISION

Is God fair? Not as we judge fairness. Thanks be to God that He is
not fair. He doesn't give us what we deserve: death and eternal damnation.
Instead, He is generous and merciful to us. He gives us Christ, our Savior.
He has forgiven us.

How do we react to those who do not yet follow Jesus?

Session 12

THE TEN VIRGINS
(Matthew 25:1–13)

FOCUS

A wedding has been planned, and all is ready. When the time comes, the bridegroom dresses in his wedding clothes and goes to the house of his bride. On the way, he is met by her attendants, who wear beautiful clothes and hold torches or lamps to light the way. The groom meets his bride, and together they go to the wedding feast. This is what a formal wedding looked like in the ancient world.

    a. What are some common wedding traditions in our culture?

    b. Which customs do we consider essential? Why?

INFORM

Read Matthew 25:1–5.

a. Who went out to see the bridegroom?

b. The bridegroom didn't come out until midnight. Did anyone expect him to come so late? What happened while they waited for him?

Read Matthew 25:6–9.

c. What did the virgins do when the bridegroom was finally about to arrive? What did the foolish virgins discover?

d. How did the foolish virgins react to their problem? What did they have to do?

Read Matthew 25:10–13.

e. What did the foolish virgins find when they returned from buying oil?

f. Why do you think the bridegroom "didn't know them"?

g. Jesus ends the parable by saying, "Keep watch, because you do not know the day or the hour." What is He trying to teach us with these words?

CONNECT

a. Jesus is like the bridegroom and we are like the virgins. We know that He is coming, but we don't know exactly when He will come. Why is He taking so long? See also 2 Peter 3:9.

b. When the bridegroom returned, the foolish virgins tried to get oil from the wise virgins. But they were not able to get any oil from them. What does this teach us about being ready for Christ's return?

c. The foolish virgins were unprepared and missed their chance to enter the wedding banquet. Will there be any second chances for those who are not prepared for Christ's return?

VISION

It's not just a story. Christ is the bridegroom who is coming, and heaven is the marriage feast. We do not want to be left out at His return. He may be taking longer than we expect, but He is coming, and He tells us to keep watch for that day.

a. How can we be prepared for His coming?

b. Like the virgins in this story, we may think that Jesus is taking a long time. How can we remain faithful and be prepared for His coming?

PARABLES OF JESUS

Session 1

READING THE PARABLES

SESSION OBJECTIVES

By the power of the Holy Spirit working through God's Word, participants will

1. describe the basic characteristics of parables;

2. understand that we can only properly understand the parables when we have faith in Christ;

3. apply these principles as they begin to study the parables.

OPENING WORSHIP

Sing "Christ Be My Leader" (*LW* 365). The second stanza highlights Jesus' teaching ministry, which we will explore in this study. After the hymn, open your study with prayer.

FOCUS

Ask a volunteer to read the Focus. Before we begin studying the parables, it may be interesting to see which parables come to mind first. You may want to look at the list of Jesus' parables found in the *Concordia Self-Study Bible*, pp. 1578–79.

INFORM

This session follows a slightly different format than the rest of the sessions. Rather than focus on one particular parable, we will look at several short parables and at other information that will help participants understand the general nature of parables.

a. Matthew 13 says that Jesus taught the people with parables. Matthew points out in verses 34 and 35 that this fulfills a prophecy from Psalm 78:2.

b. The earthly event in this parable is a woman making bread. Some other common events or activities used in the parables include planting crops, fishing, and other daily activities.

c. These three verses all show that the parables reveal truths about the kingdom of heaven.

d. A tiny amount of yeast grows to make an entire batch of bread rise. In the same way, God accomplishes amazing things with what we consider to be small. Faith grows. Christians share their faith with others. Although something may not look like much to the world, God's power truly works wonders.

e. Unbelievers hear the story, but often do not understand its meaning. Parables reveal the truth, but the truth might remain hidden from those who do not understand. Even Jesus' disciples needed Him to explain some of the parables.

f. If we want to understand the parables, we need to know Jesus. Without faith in Him, we might see the basic story, but miss the real meaning. This is a vital point.

CONNECT

a. The earthly situation is similar in both parables. A person finds something of great value and realizes that he needs nothing else. The first person finds a hidden treasure in a field. The second finds a precious pearl.

b. Many people would say that we are like the people in these parables. When we find the kingdom of heaven, we are willing to give up everything else. While it is true that we need to place the highest priority on spiritual matters, this interpretation misses an important point. We simply have not given up everything to gain heaven; instead, Christ has. He is like the man who finds a great treasure. He found us when we were still sinners and gave up everything—even His own life—to make us His. He purchased us with His own blood shed on the cross.

VISION

We receive the parables as the Word of God. That is what they are. God will use His Word to teach us, to increase our faith, and to guide us in this life.

Session 2

THE PRODIGAL SON
(Luke 15:11–32)

SESSION OBJECTIVES

By the power of the Holy Spirit working through God's Word, participants will

1. confess that we have left our Father and His will through our sin;

2. recognize our Father's unconditional love for us through Jesus Christ;

3. rejoice when others are reconciled to our heavenly Father.

OPENING WORSHIP

Our study reminds us of our sinfulness and constant need for God's forgiveness. Psalm 6 is a plea for God's mercy that He freely gives to us. Read Psalm 6, and then begin your study with prayer.

FOCUS

Ask a participant to read the Focus. Spend some time talking about strained family relationships. This common family problem is central to our study.

INFORM

This parable is filled with contrasts. The arrogance of the sons contrasts with the gentleness of their father. The rebellion of the younger son contrasts with the apparent loyalty of his elder brother. The depths of despair experienced by the young son are very different from the joys that he will experience in his father's house. So, also, our spiritual walk is one of contrasts. We sin, but God forgives. We fail, but He succeeds. We have kept grudges, but He does not remember our sins. Such great love our God has poured upon us!

a. The younger son asked for his share of his father's estate. A younger son would usually get a portion of his father's estate (though not as much as his oldest brother). A father could divide his property during his lifetime. But for a son to demand his share of the inheritance was out of line. He had no right to his father's estate—especially while his father was still living. In a way, the son told his father that he wished his father were dead!

b. The parable tells us that he traveled to a distant country and squandered his wealth in wild living. In verse 30 his brother accuses him of squandering his wealth with prostitutes. Not only was he arrogant in demanding his inheritance, he was sinful in the way he used it.

c. After spending his inheritance, he found himself in a severe famine. The only work he was able to find was feeding pigs. The Old Testament considered pigs to be unclean animals; this was one of the lowliest jobs he could get. His situation was so bad that he wanted to eat the pigs' food, but even this was denied him. He had finally hit rock bottom, and he knew it.

d. The words that describe his repentance are "he came to his senses." He finally recognized what he was doing, and he realized what he had left behind. These words are a good description of sin and repentance. Sin is senseless. It is foolish and ridiculous, but we still sin. In an instant, the younger son knew the stupidity of his sin.

e. He returned home with an attitude of humility. He knew that he had failed and wronged his father. He did not ask to return to his place as a son. "I am no longer worthy to be called your son," he said. Instead, he begged only to be treated like a servant, a hired hand.

f. Everything the father did and said was more than his son deserved. When his son was still a long way off, the father saw him and ran to meet him. He embraced and kissed his son. When the young man asked to be treated as a servant, the father chose instead to treat him as his son. He dressed him in fine clothes, put a ring on his finger (a sign of authority), and prepared a celebration feast. The son deserved none of these things. They all were part of the father's mercy and goodness.

g. The older brother was angry. He had stayed at home and been a faithful son, while his brother had wasted his inheritance. Now his brother was home and getting even more things. It just wasn't fair! The older brother was technically right. His brother had wasted his money. But the older brother had an unforgiving heart. He was not entitled to anything either! He also acted as if his father should be dead. We can understand his anger, but it was still wrong.

h. The father showed that he loved both of his sons. He told his oldest son that his inheritance was safe, and he recognized his son's loyalty to him. But he also told his son that it was right to rejoice that his brother was home and safe.

CONNECT

a. We are like the younger brother because we have run away from our heavenly Father. He has given us many blessings, but we prefer a life of sin. But God has broken through our barriers, and He has brought us back to our senses. When we confess our sins, He forgives us freely through faith in Christ Jesus and makes us His children again.

b. We are like the older brother if we look at other Christians with suspicion. Sometimes Christians expect that others will lead perfect lives, or they seem jealous of people who have lived lives of sin and then become Christians later in life. When we do this, we forget that we have all been welcomed by God's grace. None of us deserves His blessings. We cannot be angry about the forgiveness shown to others because we have received it too.

c. Our Father brings us back through the work of Jesus Christ. Because of His death and resurrection, we are forgiven. We might plead, as did the younger son, "I am no longer worthy to be called your son; treat me as one of your hired men." But God does not call us back in this way. He makes us His own children, close to His heart and loved by Him.

VISION

a. While we are rightly ashamed that we continue to sin against our God, we know that we will continue to sin. When this happens (as it does each day), we return to Christ again, letting His blood cover our sins. Our Father is constantly forgiving us!

b. We remember that we are all a part of God's family only because of His love. When others repent and believe, we rejoice with them. How wonderful that they now share the grace that has been given to us!

Session 3

THE GREAT BANQUET
(Luke 14:16–24)

SESSION OBJECTIVES

By the power of the Holy Spirit working through God's Word, participants will

1. rejoice that God has invited them to the great heavenly banquet;

2. remain steadfast in faith so that they do not reject God's invitation;

3. gladly invite others to the heavenly banquet by sharing the Gospel of Jesus Christ.

OPENING WORSHIP

This session looks at the great banquet of heaven. For your opening worship, read a prophecy of this banquet in Isaiah 25:6–9.

FOCUS

Read aloud the Focus. Discuss the invitation. Allow participants to come up with reasons not to attend. What kinds of things might keep them from this party? What would make them want to attend? As with the other parables, we can better understand this parable if we can experience the emotions of it ourselves.

INFORM

Luke 14 and 15 show Jesus dining with various people and talking about banquets and feasts. It was an honor to have a teacher like Jesus eat at your table. He would teach, share a meal, and spend time in fellowship. The remarkable thing is that Jesus did not show favoritism in His choice of table companions. In chapter 14 He eats in the house of a prominent Pharisee and teaches those in that house. In chapter 15 He welcomes sinners and eats with them. This parable shows us that God does not limit His grace, but invites all who believe in Him to the heavenly banquet.

   a. We're not told exactly how the man prepared for this banquet, but we can guess. Allow the group to speculate. If he prepared a great banquet, certainly he arranged for food and drink for his guests. He would have prepared a place for the banquet to be held and made sure that everything was just right. Whatever his preparations, we know that in the end everything was ready (verse 17).

   b. Jesus tells us that He will prepare a place for us. He does not describe all of the details, but tells us enough so that we know heaven will be a wonderful place. We also know that He has made the most important preparation. By His death and resurrection, He has forgiven us and given us a place in heaven. We will live there with Him forever.

   c. Three excuses were offered for not attending the banquet, but all of them were meaningless. One person said that he had bought a field and must go see it. Certainly he would have examined the field before buying it. The second wanted to try out his new oxen. But this also could have waited until later. The third said that his recent marriage prohibited him from attending. He could have brought his wife along. All of these excuses were very weak and insulting.

d. First, the man sent his servants out into the streets and alleys to bring in the poor, crippled, blind, and lame. These people would not often be invited to a banquet, but they were invited to this one. Then, since there was still room, the man sent his servants out of the city to find even more people. Social distinctions would not be recognized. Anyone willing to attend was welcomed to the banquet.

e. The man wanted his banquet to be full. He had taken care of all the preparations. A fine banquet was ready, and he wanted people to enjoy it. If the banquet was not full, some of his work would have been wasted.

f. We don't know how these late-invited guests reacted when they came to the banquet. They must have found it hard to believe that they were being treated so well. Other people did not invite them to banquets, but this man treated them wonderfully. They must have marveled at this wondrous banquet.

g. Those who rejected the invitation to the banquet were replaced. The master decreed that not one of those first invited would even taste the banquet. They had rejected the invitation and so would get none of the enjoyment.

CONNECT

a. Tragically, people reject God's gracious invitation to heaven. He wants all to be saved and has won the salvation of the world through Jesus' death and resurrection. But He will not force us to receive His love. Those who reject His invitation may have many reasons, but in the end their excuses are as foolish as those given in this parable. There is nothing more important than God's invitation to life eternal.

b. People offer many excuses. Allow participants to share some of these. Remember, though, that we have all failed. All of us have, at times, rejected God's invitation. We have chosen our sinful ways over His. We do not offer excuses, but a confession of our sins. God forgives us for Jesus' sake.

c. We are really members of both groups. We don't deserve a place, but God invites us anyway. We have rejected His invitation, but He forgives us through Jesus Christ and gives us a place in heaven.

VISION

Christ calls us, His people, to make disciples of all nations. Since we are still here, we know that there is still room in heaven. We are called to tell others of Christ and to extend His invitation. There are no limits to this invitation. Christ died for all, and we are privileged to share this Good News. Encourage group members to share their faith with others.

Session 4

THE TALENTS
(Matthew 25:14–30)

SESSION OBJECTIVES

By the power of the Holy Spirit working through God's Word, participants will

1. identify that God's chief blessing to us is His grace in Jesus Christ;

2. realize that God has given us gifts and talents and that He desires us to use these gifts as faithful stewards;

3. gladly and freely respond to His love with our service and witness.

OPENING WORSHIP

This parable teaches us that we are to use in an appropriate manner the gifts that God has given us. For your opening worship, sing "Take My Life, O Lord, Renew" (*LW* 404). Open your study with a prayer for God's guidance.

FOCUS

Ask a volunteer to read the Focus. Participants' responses to the questions will vary.

INFORM

In Matthew 25, Jesus gives us three distinct illustrations about the end times. The parable of the wise and foolish virgins (Matthew 25:1–13) calls us to be prepared for the coming. Matthew 25:31–46 describes Judgment Day. The parable of the talents comes between them and shows us that as we wait for the Last Day, we need to be prepared, but also live lives of active service and stewardship. As we wait for Christ's return, we carry on His work in this world.

a. The only preparations that Scripture speaks of are financial. The man entrusted his property to his servants so that they would care for it and improve it in his absence.

b. He gave them different amounts "according to their ability." He knew which servants could handle the responsibility and use the money wisely. Even the servant who failed in his responsibility had the ability to succeed.

c. We're not told what the first two servants did with the money entrusted to them. Whatever it was, they were successful. When the master returned, they had doubled the money given to them. The third servant, however, did not invest the money given to him. He buried his master's money to keep it safe. It was safe, but he did not use or improve the money given to him.

d. When the master returned, the servants were called to give an account of their stewardship. The first two servants brought back twice the money that had been given to them. The master responded by commending their work. He called them good and faithful servants. Because they had been faithful with the talents, they were put in charge of much more and they shared their master's happiness. In short, they were rewarded for their service.

e. The third servant claimed that his master was a hard man and did not want to disappoint him by losing the money. When his master returned, he gave him his money back, but he had not used or improved his master's resources. The master condemned him as lazy and wicked. He didn't even put the money in the bank where it could earn interest! The talent was taken from this man, and he was cast out.

f. It's easy to focus on the failure of the third servant, but overall the master's plan was a success. He began with eight talents and ended with fifteen. All of his servants had the ability to succeed. One failed, but the others were faithful and successful. He not only had more money, he had servants who had shown themselves to be faithful.

CONNECT

a. The "journey" is something that we live in now. The disciples saw Jesus face-to-face, but He has ascended into heaven. We know that He is with us and that He blesses us today. We also wait for His return in glory.

b. Our God has entrusted much to us. He has given us the gift of faith. He gives us all that we have and all that we are. He gives us spiritual gifts and our abilities. He gives us opportunities to serve Him. As in the parable, He expects us to use these gifts. We do not keep them to ourselves, but use them in His service.

c. In the parable, the master acted first. He chose the servants, and he gave them his money. Later, he rewarded them for their service, but they could not have done anything without his gifts and his trust. Our Christian life is similar. God has done everything for us. Most of all, He saved us through His Son's death on the cross while we were helpless sinners. He has freely given us gifts, and He empowers us to use those gifts to serve Him. Only after He has given all of this to us does He ask us to serve Him. God's gifts always come first and are always greater than our meager response.

VISION

a. Discuss together the gifts that God has given. The gift of faith has been given to all, but other gifts will vary. This is according to God's plan!

b. Here is our chance to be good and faithful servants. Empowered by the Holy Spirit, we are called to use the gifts that He has given to us. It may seem easy to hide God's gifts among ourselves, but it is God's will that we use them in service. He will aid and bless us, and He will make us good and faithful.

Session 5

THE SOWER
(Mark 4:1–9, 14–20)

SESSION OBJECTIVES

By the power of the Holy Spirit working through God's Word, participants will

1. affirm that the Bible is God's Word and that God has given that Word power;

2. realize that it is possible for Christians to fall from faith if they reject God;

3. seek to serve God in all that they do, producing a harvest for Him.

OPENING WORSHIP

A number of hymns adapt the image of this parable to music. You might want to sing "Almighty God, Your Word Is Cast" (*LW* 342) to prepare for your study. Open your study with prayer, asking God to prepare our hearts to receive the seed of His Word.

FOCUS

Ask a volunteer to read the Focus. Possible answers are as follows:

a. Often people reject God's grace.

b. The difference between Christians and non-Christians is not based on our goodness or holiness. Rather, it is a difference based simply on belief and unbelief. By God's grace Christians have not rejected Christ's mercy.

INFORM

This parable is found in the first three Gospels. See also Matthew 13:1–9 and Luke 8:1–15. All of these accounts offer not only the parable, but a direct explanation of its meaning. This explanation was requested by the disciples. In response, Jesus taught them not only about this parable, but also about the nature of all His parables.

a. The sower sows the Word of God. He represents anyone who shares God's Word with others. Ultimately, that Word comes from God Himself, but His children also sow His Word. The seed is God's Word—the Gospel of salvation through Jesus Christ. People are the ground that receives the seed of the Word.

b. In the parable, the "path" is hard ground that the seed cannot penetrate. As the seed sits on the surface, birds come to eat it. The path represents people who hear the Word, but it is immediately stolen away by Satan. They have heard but pay no attention to God's Word. It goes in one ear and out the other.

c. Grain that falls in the "rocky places" begins to grow in the shallow soil, but when the sun shines on these plants, they are scorched because they have no roots. People are like the rocky places when they receive the Word with joy but have no depth to their faith. Because of this, their faith dies away as soon as a problem comes along.

d. When the seed is planted in the thorny ground, it grows, but the thorns grow likewise. Soon the thorns choke out the good plants. While the plants are alive, they don't produce any grain, and no harvest comes from them. People are like the thorny ground when they hear the Word but allow worldly concerns to distract them. They still have faith (at least for a while), but they do nothing to help others or serve God.

e. When seed is planted in the good soil it grows and produces a wonderful harvest. People are like the good soil when they hear the Word of God, believe it, and allow God through faith to transform their lives. God works wonderful things in the lives of His people when we do not push Him away.

f. The sower freely spreads his seed over all kinds of ground. While it might seem foolish to scatter seed on paths, rocky soil, or thorny ground, the sower does so in hope of a good harvest. He isn't disappointed. The harvest from the good soil makes his efforts worth the risk. Perhaps there are small patches of good soil in the middle of the other types of soil. This image shows us how God deals with us. He doesn't just offer His Word and His salvation to certain people. God wants all to be saved, and so His Gospel is proclaimed to all—even those who might not believe.

CONNECT

a. There have been times in the past when we were like the path—hearing the Word but not receiving it. Sadly, we still may act like this at times. We choose to ignore the Word of God and so miss His blessings. Thank God that He does not give up on us!

b. God would have our faith grow! He wants our faith to have roots. We gain more depth when, by God's grace, we study and hear His Word.

c. Jesus warns us in Mark 4:19 about some of the things that can choke our faith. They are just as prevalent and dangerous today: the worries of this life, the deceitfulness of wealth, and the desires for material possessions. Anything that draws our attention away from our Savior is a thorn that threatens our faith.

d. We see the kind of "soil" that God wants us to be—good soil that produces a harvest. The way to become good soil is simply to believe— believe that Christ Jesus is our Savior who died and rose again to forgive us. When He forgives us, we are truly blessed, and He will make us into good soil. He does the work within us!

a. The crop that we produce is faith in action. By His empowering Spirit, we serve Him and other people in Jesus' name. Part of that harvest is seen as we share the Word with other people so that they too know Jesus and can serve Him. Encourage participants to be specific. What does God want to harvest from them?

b. The responsibility for sowing the seed belongs to all of God's people. Since we all have received the Word, we are all called to share the Word. God would have us tell others about the wonderful things He has done for us through Jesus Christ.

Session 6

THE UNMERCIFUL SERVANT
(Matthew 18:21–35)

SESSION OBJECTIVES

By the power of the Holy Spirit working through God's Word, participants will

1. give thanks that God has freely forgiven us and keeps no record of our wrongs;

2. forgive others in joyful response to our forgiveness in Christ;

3. understand that there are no limits to true forgiveness.

OPENING WORSHIP

As we study God's forgiveness, open by experiencing that forgiveness together. Join together in the confession of sins and declaration of God's grace from the service of Prayer at the Close of the Day (*LW*, p. 264).

FOCUS

Ask a volunteer to read the Focus.

a.- c. While we know that we are to freely forgive others, we often do not want to do so. Most people want to be forgiven, but do not want to forgive others so freely. Because of this, we might ask the same question that Peter asks in this study.

INFORM

There is a difference between some translations on the precise meaning of verse 22. Some say we should forgive seventy-seven times, others seventy times seven. This little nuance doesn't change the meaning of the text—that we should freely forgive, without keeping records.

This passage also refers to Roman money. A denarius was the average wage paid for a single day's work. A talent was valued at around 6,000 denarii. The difference in the amount of money owed by the two men could hardly be greater.

a. Peter must have thought he was being generous. To forgive someone seven times is certainly better than many people would do. But if he had to keep count, he was not really forgiving his brother.

b. Jesus said we are to forgive seventy-seven times. If we try to do this, we will lose count and fall into the habit of forgiving. Jesus gave a finite number, but really He taught that we need to keep on forgiving others.

c. The king wanted to regain his money by selling the man and his family into slavery. While this might seem barbaric to us, it was a common way of settling debts in the ancient world.

d. The man promised that if the king was patient with him, he would repay his debt. This does not seem very likely, however. It would be very difficult for him to get even a fraction of the money that he owed.

e. The king did not accept the man's offer. Instead, he forgave the debt and freed his subject. Jesus explained this generous act by simply saying, "He took pity on him." Because of the king's mercy, the man was forgiven a tremendous debt.

f. This is the disturbing part of the story. Having just been forgiven an enormous debt, the man could not treat another person with similar compassion. His debtor asked for patience and promised to repay the debt, but the man didn't listen. He had the debtor thrown into prison.

g. When the king heard about the man's actions, he confronted him: How could you not show mercy after all I have done for you? The king then treated him as the man had treated his fellow servant—the king had him imprisoned until the debt was paid. Now the man received what he had deserved.

h. Peter was acting like the man in the parable. Having been forgiven a great debt, he did not want to show that same mercy to others. Jesus told this parable to show that forgiveness does not have limits.

CONNECT

a. We owe God the enormous debt of our sins. Our rebellion against Him, our failure to do His will, and even our very nature are sinful. But God, knowing that we could never repay this debt, has taken it upon Himself. He sent His Son to be our Redeemer. Jesus paid for our debt of sins when He died on the cross for us.

b. It is true that other people sin against us. We, like Peter, may find them hard to forgive. But it is also true that we have double standards. We want to be forgiven daily, but may not want to forgive others. We hold others to a higher standard. This is not God's will for us.

c. God does not keep a record of our sins, and there is no limit to His forgiveness. He constantly forgives us for the sake of His Son, Jesus. The forgiveness never ends. So, also, we freely forgive others. In so doing, we express our gratitude to God.

VISION

a. The best motivation for our forgiveness is our awareness of how much we have been forgiven. The man in the parable was forgiven a great debt, but we have been forgiven even more. Remembering all that God has done for us empowers us to forgive also.

b. Read the statement. Allow participants time to think about how they will put forgiveness into practice.

Session 7

THE LOST SHEEP AND THE LOST COIN
(Luke 15:1–10)

SESSION OBJECTIVES

By the power of the Holy Spirit working through God's Word, participants will

1. recognize that all people are lost in sin and cannot save themselves;

2. give thanks that Christ has found us, saving us through His death and resurrection;

3. rejoice and give thanks to God when anyone is brought to faith in Christ.

OPENING WORSHIP

Begin your study with prayer. Before you study about the lost sheep, read Psalm 23

FOCUS

Read the Focus together and discuss the questions. The more participants identify with the feeling of being lost, the more powerful the parable will be.

INFORM

Luke 15 records three of Jesus' parables for us. All of them refer to things that are lost and then found. This study looks at the first two—the lost sheep and the lost coin. The third is the parable of the lost son—more commonly known as the prodigal son. That parable was studied in another session. In all of these parables, someone has lost something important, earnestly seeks it, and rejoices when it is found. So, too, our God seeks people who are lost in sin, brings them back through Christ, and rejoices when we are saved.

a. The Pharisees were angry that Jesus welcomed sinners and ate with them. They were offended that He would engage in fellowship with wicked people and even teach them. They thought that Jesus should spend His time with people who were more respectable and "holy." But they forgot that they were sinners too! Jesus came to save sinful people—that is what these parables teach us.

b. The problem was a lost sheep. The man owned one hundred sheep, and one had been lost. Even though this was only one percent of his flock, the man went to look for his lost sheep. He cared for his sheep and wanted it back.

c. The man left the rest of his flock in the open country while he searched for his lost sheep. It may seem to us that he abandoned these sheep, but they were safe. He had not left them alone: they were together, and there was safety in numbers. While the lost sheep was in great danger, the others would be safe together.

d. When he found his sheep, the man joyfully put it on his shoulders and went home. He did not yell at the sheep or beat it for running

45

away. He was happy that his sheep was safe, so he carried it home. Then he called his friends and neighbors together to celebrate. He wanted to share his joy.

e. Jesus is not really talking about sheep, but about people. God is the shepherd, and we are like the lost sheep. All human beings are lost. We have left the safety and protection of God's family to wander off into lives of sin and rebellion. Even though this is our fault, God does not abandon us but sends Jesus to this earth to find us. By His death and resurrection, He has forgiven our sins and made us His people again. Jesus has brought us back to our heavenly Father.

f. Jesus tells us that there is more rejoicing in heaven when one sinner repents than there is over ninety-nine righteous people who do not repent. God wants sinners to be saved. He does not love us because we are good or righteous by ourselves (and we are not righteous). He loves us even when we are sinners, and He makes us righteous by forgiving our sins.

g. The parable of the lost coin has the same basic message as that of the lost sheep. A woman sought her lost property and rejoiced when it was found. Jesus tells us this second parable so that we do not overlook the message. God wants sinners to be saved. He even wants self-righteous and judgmental sinners (such as the Pharisees) to be saved and know His love and forgiveness.

CONNECT

a. All people were lost in sin, and we all continue to struggle with our sinful nature and actions. We must be honest and admit that our sins are our own fault. God did not lose us—we left Him, as Isaiah reminds us. It is our own fault that we were lost.

b. The Pharisees were scandalized that Jesus spent time with sinners. Through these parables, Jesus taught them that He came to save sinners. We need to remember this as well. Christians are not perfect people who never sin. We are sinners who have been forgiven by Jesus. Since He freely forgives us, we rejoice when He freely forgives others. The only way that sinful people can be saved is if Jesus comes to them and brings them back.

c. It is truly amazing to see that even though we can never deserve God's love, Christ saves us and heaven rejoices. Jesus, our Savior, has given us worth.

VISION

a. We help them when we tell them about Jesus Christ and all He has done for them. The best thing we can do for another human being is to tell them about our Lord who has saved us and given us life.

b. We dare not be jealous or self-righteous when we see sinners repent. They receive the same blessings that we have also received. Our response is simple: when someone else believes, rejoice! We have a new sister or brother in Christ!

Session 8

THE RICH FOOL
(Luke 12:13–21)

SESSION OBJECTIVES

By the power of the Holy Spirit working through God's Word, participants will

1. affirm that we are loved and accepted by our Savior and that His success is our success;

2. place God first in their lives;

3. rejoice in God's blessings and use their possessions as faithful stewards.

OPENING WORSHIP

As you begin your study, sing or read a hymn that reminds us of the gifts that God gives us and our use of those gifts. Consider "God of Grace and God of Glory" (*LW* 398) or "Jesus, Priceless Treasure" (*LW* 270). Then open with prayer.

FOCUS

Ask a participant to read the Focus. Allow time to talk about the nature of success. Our world often defines success in terms of money or power. Sadly, we often neglect other vital things like a relationship with God or family members.

INFORM

Jesus tells this parable in response to the request in verse 13: "Teacher, tell my brother to divide the inheritance with me." This may seem like an unusual request, but it really wasn't so strange. Rabbis often were called in to settle similar disputes. If only this family had followed Scripture, they would have known that God already gave directions on how the estate was to be divided. Deuteronomy 21:17 says that the older son gets twice as much as a younger brother. Jesus, however, saw that the real problem here was not fairness or the interpretation of Scripture, but greed.

a. The man asked Jesus to intervene on his behalf with his brother. He wanted their inheritance to be divided between them. Jesus put off his question because it had already been answered in God's Word.

b. Jesus warns us against greed. He reminds us that the value of our life is not the total value of our possessions. We are worth far more!

c. The man was equating his worth with his possessions. Sadly, he had forgotten that he had many blessings from God. One of them was life itself.

d. By all outward appearances, this man was very successful. His land
    had produced a good crop. The harvest was so great that he needed
    to build new barns for storage. He had all that he needed to enjoy a
    life of ease.

e. This man told himself that he would relax once the harvest was in
    and his new barns were built. We don't know if that was really true,
    however. Greed is not easily satisfied. Once he reached his goal of
    prosperity, he might have decided that he needed even more posses-
    sions before he could relax.

f. His plan failed because he died. All of his possessions did not matter
    because he could not keep himself alive. This is why God judged him
    a fool.

g. He was rich in the eyes of the world, but that did not matter. All of
    his riches could not buy him another day of life. His greatest problem
    was that he was poor towards God.

CONNECT

a. God does not measure success by our possessions or by any other
    worldly standard. We are truly successful when we know that we are
    sinners in need of God's forgiveness and that Jesus Christ has died for
    us. We are successful when we are in Him. Our true treasures are not
    on this earth, but in heaven.

b. It is not wrong for us to have money or other possessions. These are
    gifts of God. The problem with the man in this parable is not that he
    had a good crop or that he wanted bigger barns. The problem is that
    this was all that mattered to him. He did not know the riches of a
    relationship with our gracious God.

c. We are rich towards God when we have faith in Christ. If He is our
    first priority, other things in life will be in their proper place. When
    we seek His kingdom first, other blessings will also be ours.

VISION

a. Christians remember that their possessions are all gifts of God to be
    used to His glory. We do this when we offer some of our possessions
    for use in His kingdom through our gifts and our offerings. We also
    do this when we enjoy the gifts that He has given to us. As long as we
    don't let our possessions take the place of God or other people, we
    can use them appropriately.

b. Allow participants time to reflect on this question. Most of all, we
    place God first in our lives when we believe in Him and remember all
    that He has done for us.

Session 9

THE PHARISEE AND THE TAX COLLECTOR
(Luke 18:9–14)

SESSION OBJECTIVES

By the power of the Holy Spirit working through God's Word, participants will

1. confess that no one can boast of their own righteousness because we all are sinners;

2. affirm that God forgives sinful people like us and gives us His righteousness through Jesus Christ;

3. welcome other forgiven sinners into the church with joy and gladness.

OPENING WORSHIP

The tax collector in this parable cried out to God for mercy. Sing or read together "O God of Mercy, God of Light" (*LW* 397). Rejoice in the mercy that God has shown us and enables us to show to others. Open your study with a prayer for God's guidance.

FOCUS

Read the Focus. Participants may want to add to or respond to these excuses for not going to church. Even if the reasons are faulty, they are perceived as true by many people. Perhaps some of the participants have felt this way (or still do). As you discuss the Focus questions, look for reasons for and solutions to these problems.

INFORM

It is difficult to think of two groups of people as different from each other as the Pharisees and the tax collectors. The Pharisees were respected religious leaders. People looked up to them. They tried to follow God and obey His laws. In contrast, tax collectors were hated by many people. Tax collectors collaborated with the Roman government. Many of them collected more taxes than they were required to and kept the extra money for themselves. In fact, many people hoped that the Messiah would destroy the tax collectors when He came. This parable in Luke breaks through these prejudices and shows us that God looks not at one's visible acts, but at one's heart.

a. The Pharisee thanked God that he was not like other sinful people. He reminded God of his own righteousness—he fasted and gave money. But he missed the whole point. Instead of comparing himself to other people, he should have compared himself with God's Word. If he had, he would have known that he was not righteous, that he was just like other sinful people.

b. While he might not have committed the same sins as some people, in reality he was no different. He was just as much a sinner as anyone else. He proved himself to be a hypocrite. He focused on other people's sins and excused his own.

c. Verse 11 shows us that he was really praying about one thing—himself. He wanted God to see what a wonderful person he was. Sadly, he did not understand that he was a sinner in need of God's forgiveness.

d. The Pharisee prayed to justify himself. The tax collector prayed for God to forgive him. The Pharisee stood up and made a bold show of his prayer. The tax collector stood at a distance, would not even look up to heaven, and beat his breast while he prayed for mercy. The Pharisee focused on other people's sins. The tax collector confessed his own sins.

e. Jesus tells us that God approved of the tax collector's prayer, not the Pharisee's. Jesus tells us that the tax collector went home justified before God. Remember, though, that the tax collector was not justified by his prayer. His humble prayer was an indication of his faith. He was justified by Christ.

f. The Pharisee exalted himself, but was humbled before God. The tax collector was humble, and God exalted him. The tax collector knew that he relied on God's mercy, and that was what he received.

CONNECT

a. Sadly, there are times when these words accurately describe us. All people are tempted to spiritual pride and arrogance.

b. We can't boast of our own righteousness because we don't have any righteousness of our own! Isaiah tells us that all of our righteous acts (not our worst acts, but our righteous acts) are like filthy rags. Our works are worthless before God. We cannot save ourselves.

c. We are careful not to judge others based on their sinfulness rather than on Christ's forgiveness. We are hypocrites if we rely on grace but force others to try to earn their salvation. Instead, knowing how Christ has forgiven us, we tell others that they too are forgiven.

d. Like the tax collector, we come before God in humble faith. We trust His promises, and He is gracious and merciful to us.

VISION

Spend time with your group discussing how an attitude of humbleness and faith might be nurtured in your congregation. When together we rely on Christ's grace and proclaim that we are forgiven by Him, we will welcome others to this fellowship.

Session 10

THE GOOD SAMARITAN
(Luke 10:25–37)

SESSION OBJECTIVES

By the power of the Holy Spirit working through God's Word, participants will

1. affirm that Christ loved us even when we were His enemies and still loves us;

2. be moved by the Holy Spirit to love and serve their neighbors;

3. strive to break through the barriers of sin to reach others with Christ's healing love.

OPENING WORSHIP

Like the "expert in the law" in this story, we may be tempted to ask "what must I do to be saved?" while forgetting what God has already done for us and is doing through us. Read the encouraging words found in Colossians 1:3–14. Then open your study with prayer.

FOCUS

Ask a participant to read the Focus. It's easy to give the answers that we know are right, but hard to put them into practice. Usually, we find it easiest to love the people who are most like us or most helpful to us. We find it much more difficult to love people who are antagonistic toward us or different from us.

INFORM

While this is a very familiar parable, we need to remember the context. Jesus was being tested by an expert in the Law. He clearly wanted to prove that Jesus did not know Scripture. But Jesus turned the tables on him. He told a story involving a terrible dilemma. Priests and Levites were to be ritually pure: they could not come in contact with blood. But they were also called to help others. In this parable, they must decide whether to follow the letter of the Law or help a suffering person. They choose the former. The hero of the story is an outsider—a Samaritan—who acts with compassion and truly cares for his neighbor. Through this story, Jesus challenges the "expert" and us to serve others.

a. He asked Jesus what he must do to inherit eternal life. There is nothing that we can do to inherit eternal life.

b. Jesus answered with a question, "What does the Law say?" When the man said, "Love the Lord your God with all your heart . . . and love your neighbor as yourself," Jesus told him to do this. The answer is perplexing—it's not what we would expect.

c. This is why we find Jesus' response unsettling. The man asked what he should do. Jesus told him what he had to do. But this is impossible. It is hopeless to try to save ourselves. There is nothing that we can do. Thanks be to God—He does it all for us through Jesus!

d. When they saw the wounded man, both the priest and the Levite passed by on the other side without stopping to help. They probably were trying to avoid contact with blood. Touching blood (or even worse, a corpse) would make them ceremonially unclean and unfit to serve in the temple. The problem is that they failed to help another person in need.

e. The Samaritan acted better than the others by actually helping the injured man. In fact, he did far more than we might expect. He cared for the injured man's wounds and then took him to an inn where he paid for his care.

f. The Samaritan was different because of his actions. He didn't just talk about love; he demonstrated love.

g. Allow plenty of time to discuss this question. The main theme is limitless love. We are called to serve all people without limits. This is the way God first loved us. He loved us enough to die on a cross for our sins.

CONNECT

a. While it is painful to admit the truth, we have also imposed limits. We have tried to love some people, but not all people. We have sought excuses to justify our behavior. But there is no excuse for sin.

b. Every community has their own "Samaritans." Perhaps they are people of another race, culture, or language. Maybe they come from a different class. Jesus teaches us to love and reach out to all people—not just the ones like us.

c. We may try, but we will never accomplish these things. We fail every time. But there is one who has succeeded. Jesus loves all people. He is like the Samaritan—loving those who hate Him and caring for us when we cannot care for ourselves. He died and rose again to forgive us.

VISION

a. At times people have limited God's love and their love. We have acted in ways that are inappropriate toward our brothers and sisters in Christ. Encourage your group to discuss ways we might be more open to others and ways that we might better demonstrate God's love.

b. Be specific. God wants us to love all people, but it is easy to ignore the ones we don't like. Who, specifically does God want me to love today?

Session 11

WORKERS IN THE VINEYARD
(Matthew 20:1–16)

SESSION OBJECTIVES

By the power of the Holy Spirit working through God's Word, participants will

1. remember that God has given wonderful blessings to all of us;

2. realize that we deserve none of God's blessings—He gives us what we do not deserve because of His gracious love;

3. rejoice when God gives His blessings to other believers.

OPENING WORSHIP

In this parable, we remember that God our Savior has given us work to do on this earth until Christ's return. Read Matthew 28:18–20 and open with prayer. Remember to pray for the spread of the Word of God throughout the world!

FOCUS

Ask a participant to read the Focus. Make sure that both questions are considered. Both deal with fairness. We tend to object when we think others are getting a better deal than we are, but we remain silent when we are getting more than we deserve. This is the issue addressed by this parable.

INFORM

The parables contain a number of references to money. The vineyard owner in this parable pays his workers a denarius for a day's labor. That was the standard wage for one day's work. The owner was, however, very generous in giving a full day's wage to those workers who were hired later. This is not normal behavior for an employer!

a. The vineyard owner promised the first group that he would pay them a denarius for the day. He did not make any specific financial arrangements with the workers who were hired later. He only said he would pay them what was right.

b. The vineyard owner hired his first workers early in the morning— probably around sunrise. He hired the last of his workers in the eleventh hour—about one hour before sunset. In other words, he hired workers all day long. Whenever he found unoccupied workers, he hired them.

c. When the vineyard owner began paying his workers, he began with those who had been hired last—the ones who had worked only one hour. They must have been shocked when they received a denarius, an entire day's wage, for only one hour of work.

d. We can see how those who were hired at the beginning of the day
    might have expected more. It was only fair. If the part-time workers
    received a denarius for an hour's work, then the full-time workers
    must deserve more for an entire day of labor.

e. The workers who were hired first were upset when they were paid
    only a denarius. They began to grumble against the master. They
    complained that they had done most of the work. Moreover, they
    had worked in the hottest part of the day. They deserved more!

f. It is true that the vineyard owner did not pay his employees propor-
    tionately. Yet he never broke his word. He gave the first workers what
    he had promised them. He paid the same wage to all of the workers,
    but none were cheated. Even though he was generous with the later
    workers, he still paid a fair wage to all. In fact, we might note that he
    was generous with all of the workers. All of them were hired from the
    marketplace. This was not their regular job. He gave all a chance to
    work in his vineyard, and he paid them all the same wage.

g. The story of the thief on the cross clearly shows us God's mercy. This
    man had not been a follower of Jesus, but in his last hour of life, he
    knew his Savior. Because he knew Jesus, he was saved, and we will see
    him in heaven. This man was not treated fairly—he received mercy.
    He was saved in spite of the rest of his life. This occurred because of
    God's grace and generosity.

CONNECT

a. God does bless those who come to faith later in life. The important
    thing is that we know Jesus and receive His salvation. People who
    come to faith on their deathbed are saved. So are people who have
    been Christians for their entire lives. God is generous to all who
    receive His gift of salvation through Christ.

b. This is a dangerous attitude, and one that comes from a deep misun-
    derstanding. God does bless those who come to faith later in life, but
    they have also missed a lifetime of knowing Him. They may not have
    experienced all of His blessings and had His help and support
    throughout their life. What's more, we don't know when our lives
    will end. Christ comes to us today, and He would have us know His
    love and salvation throughout our lives.

c. However long we have been a Christian, we are called to rejoice when
    another person believes. God has been merciful to us, and He will be
    merciful to others. We thank God when another child enters His family.

VISION

We are already working in our Lord's vineyard. When He touches the
hearts of other people, we dare not be jealous or envious. We rejoice that they
share the gifts that God has already given to us.

Session 12

THE TEN VIRGINS
(Matthew 25:1–13)

SESSION OBJECTIVES

By the power of the Holy Spirit working through God's Word, participants will

1. believe that we are truly prepared for Christ's return since we have faith in Him;

2. understand that there are no second chances for salvation after Christ's return;

3. look forward to Christ's return with joy and eager expectation.

OPENING WORSHIP

Sing together "Wake, Awake, for Night Is Flying" (*LW* 177). This hymn is based on the parable of the ten virgins. You may want to pray together the collect for the Sunday of the Fulfillment (*LW*, p. 94).

FOCUS

Ask a participant to read the Focus. Wedding customs in the ancient Near East were different than many of ours, but they were taken just as seriously. Briefly discuss some of our wedding customs. Which customs are considered essential? After the group has thought about wedding customs, move on to study this parable.

INFORM

One of the duties of the bride's attendants (the virgins in this parable) was that they should meet the approaching bridegroom with light. They would take torches or small clay oil lamps out into the night to light his way. Undoubtedly, all of the virgins thought they were prepared. They all came with their lamps. But when the bridegroom was delayed, we see who was truly prepared—the ones who brought extra oil. The same is true of people. Many think they are prepared for the end of the world, but only those with faith in Christ are truly ready for that day. We are wise if we trust in Him.

a. All the virgins went out to see the bridegroom. Both the foolish and the wise ones went out together, carrying burning lights. At this point in the parable, one cannot really tell the difference between the foolish and the wise.

b. It is doubtful that anyone expected his late arrival. If they had known, they would not have gone out until the time had nearly arrived. While they waited, they fell asleep and their lamps continued to burn.

c. When the bridegroom was about to arrive, all of the virgins trimmed their lamps— they made sure they were burning brightly. While doing this, the foolish virgins discovered that they had run out of oil. They were not prepared for the delay.

d. The foolish virgins had to get some oil. They asked the wise virgins, but there was no oil to spare. They were sent to purchase their own oil. Unfortunately, there were no oil shops open at midnight!

e. They found that the bridegroom had come in their absence. The wise virgins had greeted him and had entered the wedding banquet, and the door was shut. Though the foolish virgins had been invited to the wedding, they were unable to attend because they were unprepared.

f. The actions of the foolish virgins must have seemed strange to the bridegroom. He had come to his wedding banquet. The attendants had all known that he was coming. When he arrived, he went inside with his invited guests. The people who came later must have seemed like they were crashing the party. If they really knew the bridegroom, they would have been there when he arrived.

g. Jesus explains the meaning of this parable. He tells us that the wise and foolish virgins are a description of the kingdom of heaven (Matthew 25:1). Here we see that we are the virgins and Jesus is the bridegroom. We are to be prepared for His return. Since we do not know exactly when this will occur, we need to be prepared for His second coming.

CONNECT

a. Christians have often asked this question. Why is Jesus taking so long? Peter explains that He is patient with us. He is waiting for more people to believe. Thank God that He is patient with us!

b. The virgins who had prepared for the evening had enough oil. Those who were unprepared missed the wedding banquet. We are told to be ready for Christ's return. We are truly ready when we have faith in Him. But we cannot prepare for another person. Each person is called to believe. We can share our faith with them and encourage them to be prepared, but we cannot believe for them.

c. The Bible does not teach us that there will be any second chances after Christ's return. When He comes, He will judge the world. Those who believe in Him will be saved, and those who reject Him will be condemned. There are no second chances. This is why we are told to be prepared.

VISION

a. We are prepared for His coming when we have faith. Jesus has died and risen again to forgive our sins and reconcile us to the Father. We are truly ready for His return when we know that we cannot save ourselves and that we are totally dependent on Him.

b. We remain prepared by staying in the faith. God has given us much to assist us as we wait. We can trust His promises that we read about in the Bible. We can rely on His grace and forgiveness that we experienced in our Baptism. We can experience His presence in the Lord's Supper. We can share in the fellowship of His Church. We can encourage and help others in their faith. He has not left us alone; He helps us and strengthens us through the Holy Spirit.